Compassionate EVANGELISM

Steve COON

Compassionate Evangelism
by Steve Coon
Copyright © 2013

ISBN 978-1-59751-985-4

Scripture quotations in this book are taken from the King James Version of the Bible. Some Scripture quotations are paraphrased by the author.

Published and distributed by Shepherd's Voice
www.shepherdsvoice.com

Printed in the United States of America

TABLE OF CONTENTS

INTRODUCTION

If every believer in Bible-believing churches shared the gospel with one person a month, and the next month they did the same, and in addition those new believers did the same, in as little as one year the whole world will have heard the gospel!

My prayer is for every believer to simply share the good news of Jesus Christ in a compassionate, loving way with their friends and family, to allow the people to hear the good news. Jesus said, "My sheep hear my voice, I know them, and they follow Me" (John 10:27).

There is no convincing, condemning, or judging involved. You don't have to learn apologetics, or know the whole Bible, or learn a script. This is a Spirit-led and Holy Spirit-empowered event that will bring joy to you and rejoicing in heaven.

I believe even the most timid person can do this. The brand-new believer can do this. I believe that the experienced evangelist can learn to do this simply and powerfully using the Word of God.

1

GOD'S HEART
FOR THE LOST

God's heart and concern for the lost souls of the world is what the Bible is about. First of all, the Bible gives us a history lesson on man's propensity to sin. The Bible shows us the extent of what God is willing to do to redeem us from our lost condition, even when we were unaware of our situation and the terror we deserve. Through God's long-suffering, He put up with us, giving us time to repent from our ways and turn to God.

If we knew God's heart for the lost, it wouldn't do anything in us unless we were broken before God. But how can we be broken before a holy, just, loving and merciful God? The first thing we will explore is how to know God and how to be known of God.

Let's go to the first book of the Bible, Genesis, the book of beginnings.

"In the beginning God created the heaven and the earth. And the earth was without form, and void; and darkness was upon the face of the deep. And the Spirit of God moved upon the face of the waters. And God said, Let there be light and there was light. And God saw the light, that it was good: and God divided the light from the darkness. And God called the light Day, and the darkness he called Night. And the evening and the morning were the first day. And God said, Let there be a firmament in the midst of the waters, and let it divide the waters from the waters. And God made the firmament, and divided the waters which were under the firmament from the waters which were above the firmament: and it was so. And God called the firmament Heaven. And the evening and the morning were the second day. And God said, Let the waters under the heaven be gathered together unto one place, and let the dry land appear: and it was so. And God called the dry land Earth; and the gathering together of the waters called he Seas: and God saw that it was good. And God said, Let the earth bring forth grass, the herb yielding seed, and the fruit tree yielding fruit after his kind, whose seed is in itself, upon the earth: and it was so. And the earth brought forth grass, and herb yielding seed after his kind, and the tree yielding fruit, whose seed was in itself, after his kind: and God saw that it was good. And the evening and the morning were the third day. And God said, Let there be lights in the firmament of the heaven to divide the day from the night; and let them be for signs, and for seasons, and for days, and years: And let them be for lights in the firmament of the heaven to give light upon the earth: and it was so. And God made two great lights; the greater light to rule the day, and the lesser light to rule the night: he made the stars also. And God set them in the firmament of the heaven to give light upon the earth, And to rule over the day and over the night, and to divide the light from the darkness: and God saw that it was good. And the evening and the morning were the fourth day. And God said, Let the waters bring forth abundantly the moving creature that hath life, and fowl that may fly above the earth in the open firmament of heaven. And God created great whales, and every living creature that moveth, which the waters brought forth abundantly, after their kind, and every winged fowl after his kind: and God saw that it was good. And God blessed them, saying, Be fruitful, and multiply, and fill the waters in the seas, and let fowl multiply in the earth. And the evening and the morning were the fifth day. And God said, Let the earth bring forth the living creature after his kind, cattle, and creeping thing, and beast of the earth after his kind: and it was so. And God made the beast of the earth after his kind, and cattle after their kind, and every thing that creepeth upon the earth after his kind: and God saw that it was good. And God said, Let us make man in our image, after our likeness: and let them have dominion over the fish of the sea, and over the fowl of the air, and over the cattle, and over all the earth, and over every creeping thing that creepeth upon the earth. So God created man in his own image, in the image of God created he him; male and female created he them. And God blessed them, and God said unto them, Be fruitful, and multiply, and replenish the earth, and subdue it: and have dominion over the fish of the sea, and over the fowl of the air, and over every living thing that moveth upon the earth. And God said, Behold, I have given you every herb bearing seed, which is upon the face of all the earth, and every tree, in the which is the fruit of a tree yielding seed; to you it shall be for meat. And to every beast of the earth, and to every fowl of the air, and to every thing that creepeth upon the earth, wherein there is life, I have given every green herb for meat: and it was so. And God saw every thing that he had made, and, behold, it was very good. And the evening and the morning were the sixth day" (Genesis 1-31).

Notice that God did not try to convince us that He is God. He just stated the facts of His creation of the universe and all things seen and unseen.

And now here is the problem!

"Now the serpent was more subtle than any beast of the field which the LORD God had made. And he said unto the woman, "Yea, hath God said, Ye shall not eat of every tree of the garden? And the woman said unto the serpent, We may eat of the fruit of the trees of the garden: but of the fruit of the tree which is in the midst of the garden, God hath said, Ye shall not eat of it, neither shall ye touch it, lest ye die. And the serpent said unto the woman, Ye shall not surely die: For God doth know that in the day ye eat thereof, then your eyes shall be opened, and ye shall be as gods, knowing good and evil. And when the woman saw that the tree was good for food, and that it was pleasant to the eyes, and a tree to be desired to make one wise, she took of the fruit thereof, and did eat, and gave also unto her husband with her; and he did eat. And the eyes of them both were opened, and they knew that they were naked; and they sewed fig leaves together, and made themselves aprons. And they heard the voice of the LORD God walking in the garden in the cool of the day: and Adam and his wife hid themselves from the presence of the LORD God amongst the trees of the garden. And the LORD God called unto Adam, and said unto him, Where art thou? And he said, I heard thy voice in the garden, and I was afraid, because I was naked; and I hid myself. And he said, Who told thee that thou wast naked? Hast thou eaten of the tree, whereof I commanded thee that thou should-est not eat? And the man said, The woman whom thou gavest to be with me, she gave me of the tree, and I did eat. And the LORD God said unto the woman, What is this that thou hast done? And the woman said, The serpent beguiled me, and I did eat.

And the LORD God said unto the serpent, Because thou hast done this, thou art cursed above all cattle, and above every beast of the field; upon thy belly shalt thou go, and dust shalt thou eat all the days of thy life: and I will put enmity between thee and the woman, and between thy seed and her seed; it shall bruise thy head, and thou shalt bruise his heel. Unto the woman he said, I will greatly multiply thy sorrow and thy conception; in sorrow thou shalt bring forth children; and thy desire shall be to thy husband, and he shall rule over thee. And unto Adam he said, Because thou hast hearkened unto the voice of thy wife, and hast eaten of the tree, of which I commanded thee, saying, Thou shalt not eat of it: cursed is the ground for thy sake; in sorrow shalt thou eat of it all the days of thy life; thorns also and thistles shall it bring forth to thee; and thou shalt eat the herb of the field; in the sweat of thy face shalt thou eat bread, till thou return unto the ground; for out of it wast thou taken: for dust thou art, and unto dust shalt thou return. And Adam called his wife's name Eve; because she was the mother of all living. Unto Adam also and to his wife did the LORD God make coats of skins, and clothed them. And the LORD God said, Behold, the man is become as one of us, to know good and evil: and now, lest he put forth his hand, and take also of the tree of life, and eat, and live for ever: therefore the LORD God sent him forth from the garden of Eden, to till the ground from whence he was taken. So he drove

out the man; and he placed at the east of the garden of Eden Cherubims, and a flaming sword which
turned every way, to keep the way of the tree of life"
(Genesis 3:1-24).

Sin entered into the world, but remember, God is holy.
So now the problem is revealed: How can a sinful man
approach a holy God? How can he get rid of his sin so
that he can once again be in the presence of a holy God?
Let's look at v. 15 again, "And I will put enmity between
thee and the woman, and between thy seed and her Seed;
It shall bruise thy head, and thou shall bruise His heel"
(Genesis 3:15).

And here we have God's first mention of a Savior. Notice
that God didn't give any clues yet? God has spread His clues
throughout the Old Testament in prophecy after prophecy,
with a yet unstated plan at this point. His plan is hidden
through the ages, that in the ages to come He might reveal
them through His holy apostles and prophets, to make them
known to a world that is dead and on its way to hell. Now,
does God want people to go to hell? No, God created hell
for Satan and the demons that followed him in his rebellion. And now everyone who follows Satan in his rebellion
against God will spend eternity in hell. Where else is there
to go? If we do not want God's love now, God will not force
His love on us for eternity. God gives us the choice now.

But wait. If this is all, then are we all going to hell? Well,
there is more. God gave Moses the Ten Commandments.
Most people have heard of the Ten Commandments, but

actually God gave Moses over 600 different laws and ordinances. God gave them to show us how sinful we are. And to be honest, He did a complete job of it. Nobody in his right mind will deny that he has sinned. And by the way, Jesus went a little further detailing what sin is, for those of us that can make ourselves look good on the outside. Jesus shows us the problem starts in our heart and mind.

Starting in Matthew 5:28, Jesus said: "But I say unto you, that whosoever looks on a woman to lust after her hath committed adultery with her already in his heart." Jesus brings it into sharper focus. It is not just the actual doing, it's the very thought of the action. It's the thought, the lust in the mind that puts us in opposition to God.

Now we talked about Jesus a little and you might say, "Isn't He the focus of the New Testament?" Yes, He is the focus of the New Testament, but He is also the focus of the Old Testament. God foretold of Jesus' life and death and resurrection (His first coming), and His glorious return to claim the prize. It is HIStory, the story of God's amazing grace and long-suffering! The story of a loving Creator who is so amazing in His love and care for His creation that He humbled Himself to become a man, so He could claim the prize. And who or what is the prize? You, me, and every human being. So I'm the prize? Yes, you, and everybody else too. You see, when Jesus Christ died on the cross He was buying back the prized possession that was sold off over 6,000 years ago when Adam followed Satan in wanting to be like God. Yes, and He calls this prized possession His bride; the believers are called the bride of Christ.

Christ died for my sins and the sins of the whole world, right? Right. Romans 5:8 says, "But God commended His love toward us, in that while we were yet sinners, Christ died for us" (Romans 5:8). Then He said, "Believe on the Lord Jesus Christ, and you will be saved" (Acts 16:31).

So it is that simple, just believe on the Lord Jesus Christ and I will be saved? Yes, it is that simple, but it must be true belief from your heart that Jesus died for your sins and that God raised Him from the dead. Believe it so strongly that you'd do what He says. "That if you confess with your mouth the Lord Jesus, and believe in your heart that God raised Him from the dead, you will be saved" (Romans 10:9).

But what about those people that have not heard? This is the very reason I am writing this book, to encourage as many believers as I can to share the good news of Jesus Christ, as often as they can, in a loving, scriptural way. How will they hear unless someone tells them? I'm excited that you're concerned about those who haven't heard yet, because God can use you to spread the good news around.

> "For whosoever shall call upon the name of the Lord shall be saved. How then shall they call on him in whom they have not believed? and how shall they believe in him of whom they have not heard? and how shall they hear without a preacher? And how shall they preach, except they be sent? as it is written, How beautiful are the feet of them that preach the gospel of peace, and bring glad tidings of good things. But they have not all obeyed the gospel. For Isaiah said, Lord, who hath believed our report?

So then faith comes by hearing, and hearing by the word of God" (Romans 10:13-17).

My purpose is to help you hear the call of God and to equip you to tell the people around you who haven't heard the good news of Jesus Christ.

"And he said unto them, Go ye into all the world, and preach the gospel to every creature" (Mark 16:15).

"And the Spirit and the bride say, Come. And let him that hears say, Come. And let him that is athirst come. And whosoever will, let him take the water of life freely" (Revelation 22:17).

This command is for all believers. *We* are the bride of Christ, right? We will give the invitation if we are the bride of Christ. It's not about whether we have to.

"Truly, truly, I say unto you, except a corn of wheat fall into the ground and die, it abides alone: but if it die, it brings forth much fruit. He that loves his life shall lose it; and he that hates his life in this world shall keep it unto life eternal. If any man serve me, let him follow me; and where I am, there shall also my servant be: if any man serve me, him will my Father honor" (John 12:24-26).

The only person who can preach about hell is the person who shudders at the thought of anyone going to hell, who will spend time on their face crying out to God for the salvation of souls. Do not preach hell because you think you are supposed to. You will do more harm than good!

> "For God so loved the world, that he gave his only begotten Son, that whosoever believeth in him should not perish, but have everlasting life" (John 3:16).

> "The Lord is not slack concerning his promise, as some men count slackness; but is long-suffering to us-ward, not willing that any should perish, but that all should come to repentance" (2 Peter 3:9).

PEOPLE PLEASER

I must know God and want others to know Him. You might say, "I do want others to know Him; that's why I support missionaries!" That's good! But we must tell others ourselves also. That's what Jesus said. "Go into all the world, and preach the gospel to every creature" (Mark 16:15).

Now before we start condemning ourselves for not sharing the good news, let's talk about what might hinder us from sharing the gospel.

- We do not think it is good news.

- We do not know how to communicate the gospel.

• We are embarrassed by those who are always telling people, "You're sinners!" or "You're going to hell!"

• We're concerned people might think we're Jesus freaks, and we think, *Can't I just believe to myself? I mean, isn't someone's faith his own private concern?*

These are some typical responses from people pleasers. Now, I'm not condemning you; I was a people pleaser myself. But God is faithful who will give us the victory in Christ Jesus our Lord. "I can do all things through Christ who strengthens me" (Philippians 4:13). Only God can and will give us the victory!

> "For it is God which works in you both to will and to do of His good pleasure" (Philippians 2:13).

Consider these passages that discourage pleasing self or pleasing man.

> "For do I now persuade men, or God? Or do I seek to please men? For if I still pleased men, I would not be the servant of Christ" (Galatians 1:10).

> "How can ye believe, which receive honor one of another, and seek not the honor that cometh from God only?" (John 5:44).

> "Truly, truly, I say unto you, Except a corn of wheat fall into the ground and die, it abides alone: but if it die, it brings forth much fruit. He that loveth

his life shall lose it; and he that hates his life in this world shall keep it unto life eternal. If any man serve me, let him follow me; and where I am, there shall also my servant be: if any man serve me, him will my Father honor" (John 12:24-26).

"But as we were allowed of God to be put in trust with the gospel, even so we speak; not as pleasing men, but God, which tries our hearts" (1 Thessalonians 2:4).

"Even so it is not the will of your Father who is in heaven that one of these little ones should perish" (Matthew 18:14).

The *why* is found in that last verse. Think about it. If God isn't willing that any should perish, if we have put on the mind of Christ, then we shouldn't either!

"For who has known the mind of the Lord, that he may instruct Him? But we have the mind of Christ" (1 Corinthians 2:16).

As Christ is transforming us by His Spirit and through the Word of God, we put on the mind of the Spirit. For God to overcome in me the tendency to be a people pleaser, I must obey the Word and die to myself. Paul said, "I protest by your rejoicing which I have in Christ Jesus our Lord, I die daily" (1 Corinthians 15:31). Paul himself had to die daily, it wasn't a once and for all thing. So we also must die every day, and one area is the trap of pleasing people. I fought with God for years over this very item. The Holy Spirit was leading me to share the gospel on the streets again, and all I could think of was how embarrassed I would be if one of my clients saw me on the street sharing the gospel. Shame on me! How many people did I harm by living for myself? God forbid that I should do it any longer!

"For to me to live is Christ, and to die is gain" (Philippians 1:21).

I must cast myself to the wind that others may be won for Christ. Fast and pray! The time is short. There are billions of souls that have not heard the simple message of salvation through Jesus Christ. If you don't tell them, who will?

2

THE TERRORS OF HELL

People do not have any idea of how bad hell is. Even if I believe the Bible is the inspired Word of God, even if I have read through the whole Bible, I still do not understand the horrendous place called hell described in the Bible. Sometimes we read the story Jesus told in Luke chapter 16 and think, *That's not so bad!* What we do not understand is that this place in the story is hades, a place for the unsaved or unbeliever prior to Jesus Christ's death and resurrection. All that are in there will at a certain point be cast into hell or the lake of fire forever. How long could you stand in a fire? At what temperature would you try to get out? I met a man in New York City after 9/11 who had witnessed many of those who jumped off the burning Twin Towers. What kind of heat do you suppose would motivate someone to leap from over a thousand feet high? How much hotter is hell than the Twin Towers inferno? My advice is to leap into the arms of Jesus Christ, the loving Savior, who Himself took our punishment and delivered us from the wrath to come.

"For our God is a consuming fire" (Hebrews 12:29).

"There was a certain rich man, which was clothed in purple and fine linen, and fared sumptuously every day. And there was a certain beggar named Lazarus, which was laid at his gate, full of sores, and desiring to be fed with the crumbs which fell from the rich man's table: moreover the dogs came and licked his sores. And it came to pass, that the beggar died, and was carried by the angels into Abraham's bosom: the rich man also died, and was buried; and in hell he lift up his eyes, being in torments, and seeing Abraham afar off, and Lazarus in his bosom. And he cried and said, Father Abraham, have mercy on me, and send Lazarus, that he may dip the tip of his finger in water, and cool my tongue; for I am tormented in this flame. But Abraham said, Son, remember that thou in your lifetime received good things, and likewise Lazarus evil things: but now he is comforted, and thou art tormented. And beside all this, between us and you there is a great gulf fixed: so that they which would pass from hence to you cannot; neither can they pass to us, that would come from there. Then he said, I pray thee therefore, father, that you would send him to my father's house: For I have five brethren; that he may testify unto them, lest they also come into this place of torment. Abraham said unto him, They have Moses and the prophets; let them hear them. And he said, No, father Abraham: but if one went unto them from the dead, they will repent. And he said unto him, If they hear not Moses and the prophets, neither will they be persuaded, though one rose from the dead" (Luke 16:19-31).

Notice, the rich man in Abraham's bosom could see, hear, and speak. He had senses that worked; he was thirsty and he recognized Abraham and Lazarus. Interestingly, he did not ask to be taken out of the flame, he just wanted to be made more comfortable!

If you think hell isn't horrendous, if you think it is not the most violent place, then the next time Southern California is on fire, just gaze at the flaming, burning videos, and picture spending eternity in a far worse place than you could imagine.

How many times have you heard someone say, "I'm going to hell and I'm happy about it!"

I say, "Are you kidding? Why would you want to go to hell?"

"All my friends are going to be there. We will have a party and drink beer!"

Many people think hell is like coming in second place in a race, compared to going to heaven. Boy, will they be surprised.

> "For the wages of sin is death; but the gift of God is eternal life through Jesus Christ our Lord" (Romans 6:23).

"But I say unto you, That whosoever is angry with his brother without a cause shall be in danger of the judgment: and whosoever shall say to his brother, Raca, shall be in danger of the council: but whosoever shall say, Thou fool, shall be in danger of hell fire" (Matthew 5:22).

"And fear not them which kill the body, but are not able to kill the soul: but rather fear him which is able to destroy both soul and body in hell" (Matthew 10:28).

"And if your eye offend thee, pluck it out, and cast it from you: it is better for you to enter into life with one eye, rather than having two eyes to be cast into hell fire" (Matthew 18:9).

"You serpents, you generation of vipers, how can you escape the damnation of hell?" (Matthew 23:33).

"For if God spared not the angels that sinned, but cast them down to hell, and delivered them into chains of darkness, to be reserved unto judgment" (2 Peter 2:4).

"These are wells without water, clouds that are carried with a tempest; to whom the mist of darkness is reserved for ever" (2 Peter 2:17).

"Mist of darkness" means "darkest darkness, gloom as shrouded by a cloud."

> "And death and hell were cast into the lake of fire. This is the second death" (Revelation 20:14).

> "The sorrows of hell compassed me about; the snares of death prevented me" (2 Samuel 22:6).

> "The sorrows of death compassed me, and the pains of hell gat hold upon me: I found trouble and sorrow" (Psalm 116:3).

> "And shall cast them into the furnace of fire: there shall be wailing and gnashing of teeth" (Matthew 13:50).

> "The same shall drink of the wine of the wrath of God, which is poured out without mixture into the cup of his indignation; and he shall be tormented with fire and brimstone in the presence of the holy angels, and in the presence of the Lamb: and the smoke of their torment ascends up for ever and ever: and they have no rest day nor night, who worship the beast and his image, and whosoever receives the mark of his name" (Revelation 14:10-11).

"Tormented" means "torture by fire and brimstone; or flashing fire."

How can a person escape hell? By keeping the commandments? By attending church? By being good? By not believing in hell? By not believing in God?

"The fool hath said in his heart, There is no God. They are corrupt, they have done abominable works, there is none that doeth good" (Psalm 14:1).

"Jesus answered and said unto him, Truly, truly, I say unto you, Except a man be born from above, he cannot see the kingdom of God" (John 3:3).

"Jesus saith unto him, I am the way, the truth, and the life: no man cometh unto the Father, but by Me" (John 14:6).

"But as many as received him, to them gave he power to become the sons of God, even to them that believe on his name" (John 1:12).

"For the wages of sin is death; but the gift of God is eternal life through Jesus Christ our Lord" (Romans 6:23).

"Whoever resists the power, resists the ordinance of God: and they that resist shall receive to themselves damnation" (Romans 13:2).

"Likewise, you younger, submit yourselves unto the elder. Yes, all of you be subject one to another, and be clothed with humility: for God resists the proud, and gives grace to the humble" (1 Peter 5:5).

3

WHAT PEOPLE DON'T KNOW WILL KILL THEM

It is amazing to me that in Japan most people have not even heard the name of Jesus Christ, much less the gospel. What I want you to look at is how absolutely true the Word of God is. Jesus said, "My sheep hear my voice, and I know them and they follow me" (John 10:27). We met a taxi driver in a very remote area of Japan, and we shared the Word of God with him. Mind you, he said he had never heard the name of Jesus or the gospel before. But after hearing the Word of God, he received Jesus Christ into his life as his Lord and Savior. The Japanese do not have a concept of eternity. He then said, "I've been thinking about things like this." This shows me that the Holy Spirit is at work in the minds and hearts of those we minister to, before we share the gospel with them.

"Most assuredly, I say to you, he who does not enter the sheepfold by the door, but climbs up some other way, the same is a thief and a robber. But he that enters in by the door, is the shepherd of the sheep. And the sheep hear His voice. And the sheep follow Him, for they know His voice. They know not the voice of strangers. Jesus said, I am the door of the sheep: by me if any man enter in, he shall be saved. I am come that they might have life, and that they might have it more abundantly. I am the Good Shepherd; the Good Shepherd gives His life for the sheep. I am the Good Shepherd, and know my sheep, and am known of mine. I lay down my life for the sheep. Other sheep I have...and they shall hear my voice. Therefore does my Father love me, because I lay down my life, that I might take it again. My sheep hear My voice, and I know them, and they follow me. And I give unto them eternal life; and they shall never perish, neither shall any man pluck them out of my hand. My Father, which gave them me, is greater than all; and no man is able to pluck them out of my Father's hand. I and my Father are one" (John 10:1-30).

"I will declare the decree: the LORD hath said to me, Thou are My Son; this day have I begotten thee" (Psalm 2:7).

"Jesus is the firstborn from the dead" (Revelation 1:5).

"Truly, truly I say unto you, The hour is coming, and now is, when the dead shall hear the voice of the Son of God; and they that hear shall live" (John 5:25).

Over the years I have prayed for proper training in evangelism, because I surely needed it. I've made all kinds of mistakes many times over, not understanding the biblical directives for evangelism. I argued with people, used Scripture to beat them up, and tried to make them feel condemned. Then I tried the patient evangelism style, where I would wait for someone to ask me about God. No one ever did. I tried friendship evangelism where I made them think I wanted to be their friend, and then shared the gospel with them. I have handed out tracts. I used Christian rap CDs to get people's attention. I sat on benches for hours waiting for someone to sit down next to me so I could share the gospel with them. I handed out candy bars. Some of these ways worked a little, but most were doomed from the inception.

"My sheep wandered through all the mountains, and upon every high hill: yes, my flock was scattered upon all the face of the earth, and no one did search or seek after them" (Ezekiel 34:6).

"As I live, says the LORD God, surely because my flock became a prey, and my flock became meat to every beast of the field, because there was no shepherd, neither did my shepherds search for my flock, but my shepherds fed themselves and fed not my flock" (Ezekiel 34:8).

"For thus says the LORD God; Behold, I, even I will both search for my sheep and seek them out. As a shepherd seeks out his flock in the day that he is among his sheep that are scattered; so will I seek out my sheep, and I will deliver them out of all places where they have been scattered in the cloudy and dark day" (Ezekiel 34:11-12).

"LSR" LOST SHEEP RECOVERY

"I will seek that which was lost, and bring again that which was driven away, and will bind up that which was broken, and will strengthen that which was sick: but I will destroy the fat and the strong; I will feed them with judgment" (Ezekiel 34:16).

"When Jesus heard it, he said unto them, They that are whole have no need of the physician, but they that are sick: I came not to call the righteous, but sinners to repentance" (Mark 2:17).

"But when Jesus heard that, he said unto them, They that be whole need not a physician, but they that are sick" (Matthew 9:12).

"I will have mercy, and not sacrifice: for I am not come to call the righteous, but sinners to repentance" (Matthew 9:13).

God is looking for harvesters and reapers—not sod busters or people with jackhammers!

"Jesus said unto them, My meat is to do the will of him that sent me, and to finish his work. Don't say, There are yet four months, and then comes harvest? Listen, I say unto you, Lift up your eyes, and look on the fields; for they are white already to harvest. And he that reaps receives wages, and gathers fruit unto life eternal: that both he that sows and he that reaps may rejoice together. And herein is that saying true, One sows, and another reaps. I sent you to reap that whereon you bestowed no labor: other men labored, and you are entered into their labors" (John 4:34-38).

"Therefore said He unto them, the harvest truly is great but the laborers are few: pray you therefore the LORD of the harvest, that He would send forth more laborers into His harvest" (Luke 10:2).

AVOID STRIVING

I was in Norwich, England in 2007 sharing the gospel with young people, and I could see one of them being drawn by the Lord. His older sister went and got an atheist friend, and brought him over, and the atheist started insulting Jesus and God and everything else. Angry and irritated, I jumped right in defending the gospel and countering the things he was saying. The young man did not end up receiving the Lord that day, because I allowed myself to be drawn away from the simple sharing of the gospel. "And the servant of the Lord must not strive; but be gentle unto all men, apt to teach, patient, in meekness instructing those that oppose themselves; if God

peradventure will give them repentance to the acknowl-
edging of the truth; and that they may recover themselves
out of the snare of the devil, who are taken captive by him
at his will" (2 Timothy 2:24-26).

When we argue with those we are witnessing to, we are
hampering the work of God in their life. For a time, when
the Holy Spirit is convicting them, they might think of
me and even hear my voice in their head. They might even
argue with me in their mind, when in fact it is the Holy
Spirit speaking to them. If I refrain from getting into an
argument with them, then when the Holy Spirit convicts
them, it will be harder for them to ignore the Holy Spirit
and hopefully the sooner they will come to believe and
receive Jesus Christ. So it is best not to engage in an argument but give way for the Holy Spirit to speak to them.

> "To speak evil of no man, to be no brawlers, but gen-
> tle, showing all meekness unto all men" (Titus 3:2).

> "But avoid foolish questions, and genealogies, and
> contentions, and strivings about the law; for they
> are unprofitable and vain" (Titus 3:9).

> "Of these things put them in remembrance, charg-
> ing them before the Lord that they strive not about
> words to no profit, but to the subverting of the
> hearers" (2 Timothy 2:14).
> "But foolish and unlearned questions avoid, know-
> ing that they do gender strifes" (2 Timothy 2:23).

"Let your speech be always with grace, seasoned with salt, that ye may know how ye ought to answer every man" (Colossians 4:6).

"Behold my servant, whom I have chosen; my beloved, in whom my soul is well pleased: I will put my spirit upon him, and he shall show judgment to the Gentiles. He shall not strive, nor cry; neither shall any man hear his voice in the streets. A bruised reed shall he not break, and smoking flax shall he not quench, till he send forth judgment unto victory. And in his name shall the Gentiles trust" (Matthew 12:18-21).

"And the fruit of righteousness is sown in peace of them that make peace" (James 3:18).

Responding to a Bible student on how to answer questions about God, evangelist and teacher Oswald Chambers said, "Be very patient and very confident in Him. God is not a fact of common sense but of revelation. Tell him God lives—evidenced to your heart when you abandoned your right to yourself and let Him take the rule."

4

THE WORD OF GOD— USE IT OR LOSE THEIR SOUL

In the early days, we would take teams of ten to twelve people out to the streets to evangelize. And if after four or five times out together, one person would believe and receive the Lord, we would rejoice. As I prayed for God to teach me how to share the gospel more effectively, what the Holy Spirit taught me is just to do what the Word of God says. And God taught me to speak the Word of God and allow the people to just hear the Shepherd's voice. Following God's instruction I began to see five to fifteen people each day, not just hearing the gospel, but believing and receiving Jesus Christ as their Lord and Savior. The power of God in preaching the cross is in the Word of God.

At a recent beach outreach, I taught a brief twenty-minute session with a team of young evangelists. I gave each of them a copy of five Bible verses I use and said, "If you get someone to talk with you, just ask them if you could share a few things that Jesus said in the Bible. If they say yes, read the five verses and then simply ask if they want to pray to receive Jesus Christ into their life as their Lord and Savior. Then pray with them to receive the Lord." After a few hours one of the young guys came running up to me and said, "You won't believe it! I did what you said and it works! I'm a believer!" I know it works, because it is the Word of God.

Our attempts to witness by reasoning with their under-standing become useless and fruitless if we don't use the Word of God. They cannot understand or receive it because their spirit is dead. It is impossible to believe because "faith comes by hearing, and hearing by the word of God" (Romans 10:17).

> "The word which God sent unto the children of Israel, preaching peace by Jesus Christ: (he is Lord of all:) That word, I say, you know, which was pub-lished throughout all Judaea, and began from Gali-lee, after the baptism which John preached; How God anointed Jesus of Nazareth with the Holy Ghost and with power: who went about doing good, and healing all that were oppressed of the devil; for God was with him. And we are witnesses of all things which he did both in the land of the Jews, and in Jerusalem; whom they slew and hanged

on a tree: Him God raised up the third day, and showed him openly; Not to all the people, but unto witnesses chosen before of God, even to us, who did eat and drink with him after he rose from the dead. And he commanded us to preach unto the people, and to testify that it is he which was ordained of God to be the Judge of living and dead. To Him give all the prophets witness, that through his name whosoever believes in Him shall receive remission of sins. While Peter yet spoke these words, the Holy Ghost fell on all them which heard the word" (Acts 10:36-44).

Notice, "the Holy Ghost fell on all them which heard the word"—God's Word is powerful.

"Being born again, not of corruptible seed, but of incorruptible, by the word of God, which lives and abides forever" (1 Peter 1:23).

"For Christ sent me not to baptize, but to preach the gospel: not with wisdom of words, lest the cross of Christ should be made of none effect. For the preaching of the cross is to them that perish foolishness; but unto us which are saved it is the power of God" (1 Corinthians 1:17-18).

"And my speech and my preaching was not with enticing words of man's wisdom, but in demonstration of the Spirit and of power: That your faith should not stand in the wisdom of men, but in the power of God" (1 Corinthians 2:4-5).

"Now we have received, not the spirit of the world, but the spirit which is of God; that we might know the things that are freely given to us of God. Which things also we speak, not in the words which man's wisdom teaches, but which the Holy Ghost teaches; comparing spiritual things with spiritual. But the natural man receives not the things of the Spirit of God: for they are foolishness unto him: neither can he know them, because they are spiritually discerned" (1 Corinthians 2:12-14).

Preach the Word—use as few of your own words as much as possible.

"In whom you also trusted, after that you heard the word of truth, the gospel of your salvation: in whom also after that you believed, you were sealed with that Holy Spirit of promise" (Ephesians 1:13).

Preach the gospel. I should not waste my time, or someone else's time, just wanting them to think about God. People think about God all the time. Neither should I waste time just talking and using my wisdom and intellect to convince them into believing the gospel. If I can talk them into believing the gospel, then someone else can talk them into not believing the gospel. Oftentimes many use Isaiah 1:18 to say that we need to reason with unbelievers. "Come now, and let us reason together, says the LORD: though your sins be as scarlet, they shall be as white as snow; though they be red like crimson, they shall be as wool." But this particular Scripture is directed to the nation of Israel, as He is calling them back to Him.

"Who also hath made us able ministers of the new testament; not of the letter, but of the spirit: for the letter killeth, but the spirit giveth life" (2 Corinthians 3:6). This verse tells me to preach grace, not the Law. For the letter of the law kills, but the Spirit gives life. When you preach the Law, you are saying that this is the current standard. You will then measure them against the same Law to see if they are really saved. When the Law is what you're preaching, you yourself will be brought under the Law.

> "O foolish Galatians, who hath bewitched you, that you should not obey the truth, before whose eyes Jesus Christ hath been evidently set forth, crucified among you? This only would I learn of you, Received ye the Spirit by the works of the law, or by the hearing of faith? Are you so foolish? Having begun in the Spirit, are you now made perfect by the flesh?" (Galatians 3:1-3).

Jesus was crucified for our sins. The Law shows us our sins, but "by grace are you saved through faith; not of works, that no man can boast" (Ephesians 2:8-9).

> "Therefore it is of faith, that it might be by grace; to the end the promise might be sure to all the seed;

not to that only which is of the law, but to that also which is of the faith of Abraham; who is the father of us all" (Romans 4:16).

If you preach the Law, you will also start trying to live under the Law. Then you will compel others to do the same. Remember what God said through Jude.

"And of some have compassion, making a difference: and others save with fear, pulling them out of the fire; hating even the garment made unclean by the flesh" (Jude 22-23).

God's compassionate heart doesn't want you to go around blasting people, trying to convict them of their sin. It's not our job to convict people of their sin; it's the Holy Spirit's job. When they do not want to respond to the love and mercy of God, this would possibly be a time to tell them about the terrors of hell, but only as the Holy Spirit leads and with a compassionate heart.

"Nevertheless I tell you the truth; It is expedient for you that I go away: for if I go not away, the Comforter will not come unto you; but if I depart, I will send him unto you. And when he is come, he will reprove the world of sin, and of righteousness, and of judgment" (John 16:7-8).

We are to use hell as the fear factor, not the Law—and only if they will not respond to the grace of God. What if you are always preaching the Law and someone thinks,

Wow, I'll have to try harder to keep the Law, because I'm not measuring up? If you are preaching the Law, you are saying that keeping the Law will get them to heaven. You are baiting them into thinking that if they just work harder they'll be okay.

> "For I am not ashamed of the gospel of Christ: for it is the power of God unto salvation to every one that believeth; to the Jew first, and also to the Greek" (Romans 1:16).

> "Faith cometh by hearing, and hearing by the word of God" (Romans 10:17).

> "Preach the word; be instant in season, out of season; reprove, rebuke, exhort with all longsuffering and doctrine" (2 Timothy 4:2).

> "Therefore they that were scattered abroad went everywhere preaching the word. Then Philip opened his mouth, and began at the same scripture, and preached unto him Jesus" (Acts 8:4, 35).

> "Now when the apostles which were at Jerusalem heard that Samaria had received the word of God, they sent unto them Peter and John" (Acts 8:14).

> "And they, when they had testified and preached the word of the Lord, returned to Jerusalem, and preached the gospel in many villages of the Samaritans" (Acts 8:25).

"And he commanded us to preach unto the people, and to testify that it is he which was ordained of God to be the Judge of living and dead" (Acts 10:42).

"Of his own will begat he us with the word of truth, that we should be a kind of firstfruits of his creatures" (James 1:18).

"Wherefore lay apart all filthiness and superfluity of naughtiness, and receive with meekness the engrafted word, which is able to save your souls" (James 1:21).

"Being born again, not of corruptible seed, but of incorruptible, by the word of God, which lives and abides forever" (1 Peter 1:23).

"But the word of the Lord endures forever. And this is the word which by the gospel is preached unto you" (1 Peter 1:25).

Do not just say nice things about Jesus like, "God loves you." Don't just invite them to church or an outreach. Preach the gospel to them. That way, if they find themselves dying tonight, they will have heard the Word of God, and the Holy Spirit can draw them to salvation.

"How then shall they call on him in whom they have not believed? and how shall they believe in him of whom they have not heard? and how shall they hear without a preacher? And how shall they preach, except they be sent? as it is written, How beautiful are the feet of them that preach the gospel of peace, and bring glad tidings of good things! But they have not all obeyed the gospel. For Isaiah saith, Lord, who hath believed our report? So then faith cometh by hearing, and hearing by the word of God" (Romans 10:14-17).

"Neither pray I for these alone, but for them also which shall believe on me through their word" (John 17:20).

"For after that in the wisdom of God the world by wisdom knew not God, it pleased God by the foolishness of preaching to save them that believe" (1 Corinthians 1:21).

"For this cause also thank we God without ceasing, because, when ye received the word of God which ye heard of us, ye received it not as the word of men, but as it is in truth, the word of God, which effectually works also in you that believe" (1 Thessalonians 2:13).

"For the word of God is alive, and powerful, and sharper than any two-edged sword, piercing even to the dividing asunder of soul and spirit, and of the joints and marrow, and is a discerner of the thoughts and intents of the heart" (Hebrews 4:12).

It is very important to use the Word of God, but when using the Word of God, we need to say it with proper inflection. This is helpful to the hearer. Don't rush through the Scriptures. Remember, it's the Word of God and it doesn't return void. Also, when sharing Scriptures, don't feel like you have to give the Scripture reference because you will just confuse them. It is the Word of God that doesn't return void, not the location in the Bible.

When sharing with someone, I have learned not to allow myself to be interrupted. I deliver the whole message and if they have a question, I just put my hand up with a "wait" gesture. By the end of my message, usually in three to five minutes, most of their questions have been answered. I also make a point not to give my personal opinion. Often, speaking God's Word from God's heart is sufficient to allow His love to flow to the people I'm talking to. And finally, I keep in mind not to go off on a pet peeve or something that I think will impress them. After all, I do not want them to remember me, I want them to remember Jesus Christ and Him crucified!

> "For my thoughts are not your thoughts, neither are your ways my ways, says the LORD. For as the heavens are higher than the earth, so are my ways higher than your ways, and my thoughts than your thoughts. For as the rain comes down, and the snow from heaven, and returns not there, but it waters the earth, and makes it bring forth and bud, that it may give seed to the sower, and bread to the eater: So shall my word be that goes forth out of my mouth:

it shall not return unto me void, but it shall accomplish that which I please, and it shall prosper in the thing whereto I sent it" (Isaiah 55:8-11).

"For the hope which is laid up for you in heaven, whereof you heard before in the word of the truth of the gospel; which is come unto you, as it is in all the world; and brings forth fruit, as it does also in you, since the day you heard of it, and knew the grace of God in truth" (Colossians 1:5-6).

"For our gospel came not unto you in word only, but also in power, and in the Holy Ghost, and in much assurance; as you know what type of men we were among you for your sake" (1 Thessalonians 1:5).

"Of his own will begat he us with the word of truth, that we should be a kind of firstfruits of his creatures" (James 1:18).

"And receive with meekness the engrafted word, which is able to save your souls" (James 1:21b).

"Therefore they that were scattered abroad went everywhere preaching the word" (Acts 8:4).

"Now when the apostles which were at Jerusalem heard that Samaria had received the word of God, they sent unto them Peter and John" (Acts 8:14).

"And they, when they had testified and preached the word of the Lord, returned to Jerusalem, and preached the gospel in many villages of the Samaritans" (Acts 8:25).

"Then Philip opened his mouth, and began at the same scripture, and preached unto him Jesus" (Acts 8:35).

"And as they went on their way, they came unto a certain water: and the eunuch said, See, here is water; what does hinder me to be baptized? And Philip said, If thou believe with all your heart, you may. And he answered and said, I believe that Jesus Christ is the Son of God. And he commanded the chariot to stand still: and they went down both into the water, both Philip and the eunuch; and he baptized him. And when they were come up out of the water, the Spirit of the Lord caught away Philip, that the eunuch saw him no more: and he went on his way rejoicing" (Acts 8:36-39).

"In whom you also trusted, after that you heard the word of truth, the gospel of your salvation: in whom also after that you believed, you were sealed with the Holy Spirit of promise" (Ephesians 1:13).

"But hath in due times manifested his word through preaching, which is committed unto me according to the commandment of God our Savior" (Titus 1:3).

"Let your speech be always with grace, seasoned with salt, that ye may know how you ought to answer every man" (Colossians 4:6).

"And such trust have we through Christ to God-ward: not that we are sufficient of ourselves to think anything as of ourselves; but our sufficiency is of God; who also hath made us able ministers of the new testament; not of the letter, but of the spirit: for the letter kills, but the spirit gives life" (2 Corinthians 3:4-6)

Remember, we are to preach the grace of God, not the Law. The Law is the seasoning, not the main course. People already know they are sinners. The ones that will affirm they are not sinners are the self-righteous Pharisee types. I find very few people like that, maybe one out of 2,000 or 3,000 people that I share the gospel with, at the most. How we present the gospel can make a big difference. If you say, "You're a sinner," you put them on the defensive. They think you are judging or condemning them. Instead I say, "We have all sinned," showing that I am in the same boat as them, and that I also need a Savior.

Now there was one exception. In Cork City, Ireland a few years ago, I was in the shopping area preaching to whoever would talk to me. A group of five schoolgirls around fourteen years old were hearing the gospel, and at the mention of Christ dying for our sins, four of the girls pointed to the fifth girl and said that she has not sinned. I turned to the fifth girl, "So you have never sinned, even once in your life?"

She answered very humbly and sheepishly, "No, sir, I haven't sinned."

I asked her to stand to the side, and I would talk to her in a few minutes. I completed preaching to the four girls and asked them if they wanted to go to heaven when they died, and they all affirmed yes. So I invited them to pray a prayer with me, asking God to forgive them for their sins and for Jesus to come live in them and be their Lord and Savior. After they prayed and I gave them the basic "Now that you are walking with God" instructions, I talked with the fifth girl.

"Have you ever broken any of the commandments of God?"

She very politely said no, she could not ever remember breaking one of the commandments. Now this girl was so innocent looking, I thought, *If I ever met someone who had not sinned, they could not have looked any more innocent than this girl!* I said to her that it was not my intention to hurt her feelings or to make her feel bad, but what I was going to say would be very painful for her to hear. She said okay.

"Have you ever had a friend do something really stupid, and at a later time, someone asked you about the situation, and you, to try to protect your friend's reputation, said a little white lie, and said, 'No, she did not do that!'?"

At this point, she started to cry profusely and asked, "Is that a sin too?"

I said, "Yes, anything, a thought, word, or deed that breaks any of God's commandments is sin!"

I then preached the gospel to her and she believed and received Jesus Christ into her life. She very eagerly prayed with me to receive Jesus as her Lord and Savior. The point is that most people know that they sin, but it is the Holy Spirit's job to convict the world of sin. Jesus said, "When He has come, He will convict the world of sin, and of righteousness, and of judgment" (John 16:8).

"But he gives more grace. Wherefore he said, God resists the proud, but gives grace unto the humble" (James 4:6).

God is the one to break the proud. I cannot, nor should I try.

5

FULL POWER AND ANOINTING OF GOD

On a recent trip, we were going into the countryside of Haiti to do children's ministry outreaches. Kirby, my translator, and I had to ride four *taptaps* to get to the area. A "taptap" is a Toyota truck that has been converted into a taxi and can carry up to twenty people. We left at 7:45 a.m. and arrived about three hours later because these taxis would typically pick up passengers along the way. While on board these taptaps, Kirby and I started to share the gospel with the passengers. On the first one we shared with about fifteen people and they all received the Lord. The second one had about thirteen people and they all believed and received the Lord also. The third one was a bus and there were about seventy people on board. Praise the Lord, all received the Word of God with joy and accepted the Lord. But the last one had twenty people and most of them were hotly arguing with each other. So we prayed for the Holy Spirit to fall on this taptap, and bring God's peace. Soon they quieted down and we were able to share the gospel. The Holy Spirit fell on everyone on the bus and after they all received the Lord, the guy next to me then gave his testimony. We were able to give them much exhortation and encouragement. All together that morning we shared with about 120 people while on our way to minister at the outreaches. Though we arrived late, we still had time to share the gospel with about a hundred kids at the first location—and help feed them lunch—and with another seventy kids at the second location. Praise the Lord. What a day of seeing the power of God at work!

> "The Spirit of the Lord is upon me, because he has anointed me to preach the gospel to the poor; he has sent me to heal the brokenhearted, to preach deliverance to the captives, and recovering of sight to the blind, to set at liberty them that are bruised, to preach the acceptable year of the Lord" (Luke 4:18-19).

> "Jesus said unto them, My meat is to do the will of him that sent me, and to finish his work. Do not say, There are yet four months, and then comes the harvest? Behold, I say unto you, lift up your eyes, and look on the fields; for they are white already to harvest! And he that reaps receives wages, and

gathers fruit unto life eternal: that both he that sows and he that reaps may rejoice together. And herein is that saying true, 'One sows, and another reaps.' I sent you to reap that whereon you bestowed no labor: other men labored, and you are entered into their labors" (John 4:34-38).

Take note in v. 37, Jesus is commissioning us to reap. If Jesus sends us, He will surely give us the equipping for the task. We cannot be effective in our own power and determination. We must walk in the power and demonstration of the Holy Spirit.

"Such trust have we through Christ to God-ward: not that we are sufficient of ourselves to think anything as of ourselves; but our sufficiency is of God; who also hath made us able ministers of the new testament; not of the letter, but of the spirit: for the letter kills, but the spirit gives life" (2 Corinthians 3:4-6).

Now you may ask: How can I do these things? The truth is you cannot. You do not have the capacity or power to do what God asks you to do. Look at Peter.

"Then Peter took him, and began to rebuke him, saying, Be it far from you, Lord: this shall not be unto you. But He turned, and said unto Peter, Get behind me, Satan: you are an offence to me: for you do not savor the things that are of God, but those that are of men" (Matthew 16:22-23).

Peter did not have it all together, nor did he act in a spiritual way. He rebuked Jesus for telling them that He was going to die for their sins and the sins of the whole world. Can you imagine rebuking Jesus for telling about God's plan for the redemption of the whole human race? What was Peter lacking? Peter was lacking the power of the Holy Spirit through the baptism or empowerment of the Holy Spirit.

Jesus made a promise in Acts 1:8, "But you will receive power after the Holy Ghost is come upon you and you will be witnesses unto me both in Jerusalem, Judea, and in Samaria, and unto the uttermost part of the earth."

> "And when the day of Pentecost was fully come, they were all with one accord in one place. And suddenly there came a sound from heaven as of a rushing mighty wind, and it filled the whole house where they were sitting. And there appeared to them cloven tongues like as of fire, and it sat upon each of them. And they were all filled with the Holy Ghost, and began to speak with other tongues, as the Spirit gave them utterance" (Acts 2:1-4).

These men who were afraid of the Jews since the death and resurrection of Jesus, who were afraid to go out in public and admit that they were followers of Jesus Christ, Peter himself denying the Lord three times now, to them an astonishing thing happened.

> "Others mocked said, 'These men are full of new wine.' But Peter, standing up with the eleven,

lifted up his voice, and said unto them, You men of Judaea, and all you that dwell at Jerusalem, be this known unto you, and hearken to my words: For these are not drunken, as you suppose, seeing it is but the third hour of the day. But this is that which was spoken by the prophet Joel; And it shall come to pass in the last days, says God, I will pour out of my Spirit upon all flesh: and your sons and your daughters shall prophesy, and your young men shall see visions, and your old men shall dream dreams: And on my servants and on my handmaidens I will pour out in those days of my Spirit; and they shall prophesy: And I will show wonders in heaven above, and signs in the earth beneath; blood, and fire, and vapor of smoke: The sun shall be turned into darkness, and the moon into blood, before that great and notable day of the Lord come: And it shall come to pass, that whosoever shall call on the name of the Lord shall be saved. You men of Israel, hear these words; Jesus of Nazareth, a man approved of God among you by miracles and wonders and signs, which God did by him in the midst of you, as ye yourselves also know: Him, being delivered by the determinate counsel and foreknowledge of God, you have taken, and by wicked hands have crucified and slain: Whom God hath raised up, having loosed the pains of death: because it was not possible that he should be held by it. For David spoke concerning him, I foresaw the Lord always before my face, for he is on my right hand, that I should not be moved: Therefore did my heart rejoice, and my tongue was glad; moreover also my flesh shall rest in hope: Because you wilt not leave my soul in hell, neither wilt thou suffer your Holy One to see corruption. Thou hast made known to me the ways of life; thou shalt make me full of joy with thy countenance. Men and brethren, let me freely speak unto you of the patriarch David, that he is both dead and buried, and his sepulchre is with us unto this day. Therefore being a prophet, and knowing that God had sworn with an oath to him, that of the fruit of his loins, according to the flesh, he would raise up Christ to sit on his throne; He seeing this before spoke of the resurrection of Christ, that his soul was not left in hell, neither his flesh did see corruption. This Jesus hath God raised up, whereof we all are witnesses. Therefore being by the right hand of God exalted, and having received of the Father the promise of the Holy Ghost, he has shed forth this, which ye now see and hear. For David is not ascended into the heavens: but he says himself, The LORD said unto my Lord, Sit thou on my right hand, Until I make your foes your footstool. Therefore let all the house of Israel know assuredly, that God hath made that same Jesus, whom you have crucified, both Lord and Christ. Now when they heard this, they were pricked in their heart, and said unto Peter and to the rest of the apostles, Men and brethren, what shall we do? Then Peter said unto them, Repent, and be baptized every one of you in the name of Jesus Christ for the remission of sins, and ye shall receive the gift of the Holy Ghost. For the promise is unto you, and to your children, and to all that are afar off, even as many as the Lord our God shall call. And with many other words did he testify and exhort, saying, Save yourselves from this crooked generation. Then they that gladly received his word were baptized: and the same day there were added unto them about three thousand souls" (Acts 2:13-41).

The difference is the power of the Holy Spirit—God's powerful Word, working in us and through us.

"And my speech and my preaching was not with enticing words of man's wisdom, but in demonstration of the Spirit and of power: That your faith should not stand in the wisdom of men, but in the power of God" (1 Corinthians 2:4-5).

"And when they heard that, they lifted up their voice to God with one accord, and said, Lord, you are God, which hast made heaven, and earth, and the sea, and all that in them is: Who by the mouth of thy servant David did said, Why did the heathen rage, and the people imagine vain things? The kings of the earth stood up, and the rulers were gathered together against the Lord, and against his Christ. For of a truth against thy Holy child Jesus, whom thou hast anointed, both Herod, and Pontius Pilate, with the Gentiles, and the people of Israel, were gathered together, For to do whatsoever your hand and your counsel determined before to be done. And now, Lord, behold their threats: and grant unto your servants, that with all boldness they may speak thy word, By stretching forth your hand to heal; and that signs and wonders may be done by the name of thy Holy servant Jesus. And when they had prayed, the place was shaken where they were assembled together; and they were all filled with the Holy Ghost, and they spoke the word of God with boldness" (Acts 4:24-31).

BE LED BY GOD'S SPIRIT

"I will instruct you and teach you in the way which you shalt go: I will guide you with my eye" (Psalm 32:8).

If you want to be used of God, you need to let God's Word live in you. Get up early and spend time alone with God, before things start moving around at home. Pray before you read God's Word for Him to speak to you. And listen to His still small voice. Get on your knees or face before God. Humble yourself in the sight of the Lord and He shall lift you up. Have daily fellowship with the Lord. Praise Him and thank Him for everything all day, for this is the will of God in Christ Jesus concerning you. Be on fire with the humility and joy of the Lord, for the joy of the Lord is your strength.

God will draw sinners to Himself through your zeal for Him. Remember when Moses was in the backside of the desert, and he stopped to see a sight. The sight was a bush that was burning. This was a common sight in the desert. Some of the bushes in the desert would spontaneously light on fire because of the intense heat. What was different about this burning bush from other burning bushes that Moses had seen in the desert? Even though it burned, it was not consumed. Be on fire for God by His Spirit; let your light shine brightly for Him and you will not be consumed.

> "Restore unto me the joy of thy salvation; and uphold me with thy free spirit. Then will I teach transgressors thy ways; and sinners shall be converted unto thee" (Psalms 51:12-13).

You see, we weren't even looking for God. God is looking for us!

> "But Isaiah is very bold, and said, I was found of them that sought me not; I was made manifest unto them that asked not after me. But to Israel he said, All day long I have stretched forth my hands unto a disobedient and gainsaying people" (Romans 10:20-21).

> "I am sought of them that asked not for me; I am found of them that sought me not: I said, Behold me, behold me, unto a nation that was not called by my name. I have spread out my hands all the day unto a rebellious people, which walked in a way that was not good, after their own thoughts" (Isaiah 65:1-2).

6

PRAYER PREPARATION

"And I will give unto thee the keys of the kingdom of
heaven: and whatsoever thou shalt bind on earth shall
be bound in heaven: and whatsoever thou shalt loose
on earth shall be loosed in heaven" (Matthew 16:19).

The keys to the kingdom lies in prayer preparation or inter-
cession, binding and loosing. Not that I would bind or
loose, but that I would pray, "Lord, please bind the works
of darkness in this person's life" or "Lord, please loose that
person from the works of the enemy."

The power is not in the prayer. The power is in the One
we are praying to.

"Yet Michael the archangel, when contending with
the devil he disputed about the body of Moses,
dared not bring against him a railing accusation,
but said, The Lord rebuke you" (Jude 9).

"Truly, I say unto you, Whatsoever ye shall bind on earth shall be bound in heaven: and whatsoever ye shall loose on earth shall be loosed in heaven. Again I say unto you, That if two of you shall agree on earth as touching any thing that they shall ask, it shall be done for them of my Father which is in heaven. For where two or three are gathered together in my name, there am I in the midst of them" (Matthew 18:18-20).

"And from the days of John the Baptist until now the kingdom of heaven suffers violence, and the violent take it by force" (Matthew 11:12).

We must pray specifically for their soul, not just, "God, please save them," but asking God to bind every power that would bind their mind and heart. We need to come in prayer against everything that would come between them and receiving the Lord, interceding before God to show them how good He is, and to reveal Himself to them. We must violently intercede for the saved and the unsaved. We must pray as if we were in hand-to-hand combat for the life of the ones we love, using every advantage at our disposal.

We need to cry out to the Lord in faith, believing Him for His promises to save all who will call upon the name of the Lord. What and when and how should I pray?

• I pray for the unsaved when I wake up during the night.

• I pray for the unsaved when I wake up in the morning.

• I pray for the lost during the day.

• I pray for God to set up divine appointments.

• I pray for God to prepare hearts to hear the Word and to believe.

• I pray for God to search me and know me, to try my ways, to see if there is any wicked way in me and to lead me in the way everlasting.

• I pray for God to make the soil of my soul into that good soil that brings forth thirty, sixty, a hundredfold.

• I pray for God to grant unto His servant that with all boldness I may speak His Word, for Him to stretch forth His hand to heal the sick, that signs and wonders may be done by His holy servant Jesus Christ.

> "No man can enter into a strong man's house, and spoil his goods, except he will first bind the strong man; and then he will spoil his house" (Mark 3:27).

> "Confess your faults one to another, and pray one for another, that ye may be healed. The effectual fervent prayer of a righteous man avails much. Elias was a man subject to like passions as we are, and he prayed earnestly that it might not rain: and it rained not on the earth by the space of three years and six months. And he prayed again, and the heaven gave rain, and the earth brought forth her fruit" (James 5:16-18).

7

THE LAW
OR GRACE

"It's my duty to convict the sinner of his sin. Man, he needs to admit that he is a dirty, rotten sinner!"

"Hey! God loves you. We are all His children!"

Which of these statements is correct? Neither. Both are off base and unscriptural. The first statement has someone taking on the role of the Holy Spirit in convicting a person of sin. The attitude of the heart is off. We are to put on the mind of Christ. God is not into having us grovel. The second statement is also incorrect in that it has not given the problem nor the solution. But this Scripture includes the problem and the solution: "For God so loved the world, that he gave his only begotten Son, that whosoever believeth in him should not perish, but have everlasting life" (John 3:16).

"Nevertheless I tell you the truth; it is expedient for you that I go away: for if I go not away, the Comforter will not come unto you; but if I depart, I will send him unto you. And when he is come, he will reprove the world of sin, and of righteousness, and of judgment" (John 16:7-8).

"Then answered them the Pharisees, Are ye also deceived? Have any of the rulers or of the Pharisees believed on him? But this people who do not know the law are cursed" (John 7:47-49).

It seems to be Pharisaical to think that by teaching or preaching the Law it will change someone's behavior. I'm not saying not to use the Law ever, what I'm saying is to use it lawfully. Remember, to the Jews Moses was preached every Sabbath day. So if you preach the Law, you too will bring yourself under the Law, and become as the self-righteous Pharisees. Instead, use the Law to show them that no one can follow the Law. It is only our schoolmaster to bring us to Christ for salvation.

"Wherefore the law was our schoolmaster to bring us unto Christ, that we might be justified by faith. But after that faith is come, we are no longer under a schoolmaster. For you are all the children of God by faith in Christ Jesus" (Galatians 3:24-26).

Remember we are saved by grace through faith; it is the gift of God!

"For by grace are you saved through faith; and that not of yourselves: it is the gift of God: not of works, lest any man should boast" (Ephesians 2:8-9).

Nowhere did Jesus humiliate anyone by having them publicly renounce their sins, or saying they are a lying, thieving, blaspheming adulterer. Even though all this is true, and our sins are exceedingly multiplied beyond this, we are not instructed to publicly confess our sins. We are instructed to confess our belief in our Lord Jesus Christ.

"That if you shalt confess with your mouth the Lord Jesus, and shalt believe in your heart that God hath raised him from the dead, you shalt be saved. For with the heart man believeth unto righteousness; and with the mouth confession is made unto salvation. For the scripture says, Whosoever believes on him shall not be ashamed" (Romans 10:9-11).

"And that every tongue should confess that Jesus Christ is Lord, to the glory of God the Father" (Philippians 2:11).

"Whosoever therefore shall confess me before men, him will I confess also before my Father which is in heaven. But whosoever shall deny me before men, him will I also deny before my Father which is in heaven" (Matthew 10:32-33).

"Also I say unto you, Whosoever shall confess me before men, him shall the Son of man also confess before the angels of God: but he that denies me before men shall be denied before the angels of God" (Luke 12:8-9).

"Keep yourselves in the love of God, looking for the mercy of our Lord Jesus Christ unto eternal life. And of some have compassion, making a difference: and others save with fear, pulling them out of the fire; hating even the garment spotted by the flesh" (Jude 21-23).

So for the majority we preach the Word with an abundance of grace. And for others, we "save with fear, pulling them out of the fire." "Save with fear" means to use the fear of hell in trying to get them saved.

"For the law was given by Moses, but grace and truth came by Jesus Christ" (John 1:17).

Remember we are to preach the good news of the gospel. We are not called to preach the Law, but grace. The Law is not good news—grace is good news!

8

REPENTANCE

There seems to be some confusion about repentance when a person gets saved. Some tend to think a person has to be sorry for their sins and promise God never to sin again before they can be saved. Let's look at the meaning of repentance from *Vine's Expository Dictionary.*

A. Verb

1. *metanoeo* NT:3340, lit., "to perceive afterwards" (*meta*, "after," implying "change," *noeo*, "to perceive"; *nous*, "the mind, the seat of moral reflection"), in contrast to *pronoeo*, "to perceive beforehand," hence signifies "to change one's mind or purpose," always, in the NT, involving a change for the better, an amendment, and always, except in Luke 17:3,4, of "repentance" from sin. The word is found in the Synoptic Gospels (in Luke, nine times), in Acts five times, in the

Apocalypse twelve times, eight in the messages to the churches, 2:5 (twice), 16,21 (twice), RV, "she willeth not to repent" (2nd part); 3:3,19 (the only churches in those chapters which contain no exhortation in this respect are those at Smyrna and Philadelphia); elsewhere only in 2 Cor. 12:21. See also the general Note below.

2. *metamelomai* NT:3338, *meta*, as in No. 1, and *melo*, "to care for," is used in the passive voice with middle voice sense, signifying "to regret, to repent oneself," Matt. 21:29, RV, "repented himself"; v. 32, RV, "ye did (not) repent yourselves" (KJV, "ye repented not"); 27:3, "repented himself"; 2 Cor. 7:8 (twice), RV, "regret" in each case; Heb. 7:21, where alone in the NT it is said (negatively) of God.

B. Adjective

ametameletos NT:278, "not repented of, unregretted" (a, negative, and a verbal adjective of A, No. 2), signifies "without change of purpose"; it is said (a) of God in regard to his "gifts and calling," Rom. 11:29; (b) of man, 2 Cor. 7:10, RV, "[repentance (*metanoia*, see C)]... which bringeth no regret" (KJV, "not to be repented of"); the difference between *metanoia* and *metamelomai*, illustrated here, is briefly expressed in the contrast between "repentance" and "regret."

C. Noun

metanoia NT:3341, "afterthought, change of mind, repentance," corresponds in meaning to A, No. 1, and is used of "repentance" from sin or evil, except in Heb. 12:17, where the word "repentance" seems to mean, not simply a change of Isaac's mind, but such a change as would reverse the effects of his own previous state of mind. Esau's birthright-bargain could not be recalled; it involved an irretrievable loss.

As regards "repentance" from sin, (a) the requirement by God on man's part is set forth, e. g., in Matt. 3:8; Luke 3:8; Acts 20:21; 26:20; (b) the mercy of God in giving "repentance" or leading men to it is set forth, e. g., in Acts 5:31; 11:18; Rom. 2:4; 2 Tim. 2:25. The most authentic mss. omit the word in Matt. 9:13 and Mark 2:17, as in the RV.

Note: In the OT, "repentance" with reference to sin is not so prominent as that change of mind or purpose, out of pity for those who have been affected by one's action, or in whom the results of the action have not fulfilled expectations, a "repentance" attributed both to God and to man, e. g., Gen. 6:6; Ex. 32:14 (that this does not imply anything contrary to God's immutability, but that the aspect of His mind is changed toward an object that has itself changed, see under RECONCILE).

In the NT the subject chiefly has reference to "repentance" from sin, and this change of mind involves both a turning from sin and a turning to God, <u>but turning to God is first and paramount</u>! The parable of the Prodigal Son is an outstanding illustration of this. Christ began His ministry with a call to "repentance," Matt. 4:17, but the call is addressed, not as in the OT to the nation, but to the individual. In the Gospel of John, as distinct from the Synoptic Gospels, referred to above, "repentance" is not mentioned, even in connection with John the Baptist's preaching; in John's gospel and 1st epistle the effects are stressed, e. g., in the new birth, and, generally, in the active turning from sin to God by the exercise of faith John 3:3; 9:38; 1 John 1:9, as in the NT in general.[1]

Occasionally after a new believer has come to the Lord, a brother or sister will ask me, "Did they repent of all their sins? I mean, did they promise they aren't going to do those sins anymore?" And what they are asking is whether that new believer has renounced all of their sins before they asked Jesus to be their Lord and Savior. My question is, "Have you stopped sinning?" Well, I haven't yet. I mean I'm not happy about it, but I still fall short. If I were to think that God requires me, by my own determination, to stop sinning before I can be saved, then we would all be hopelessly lost! Sure, I can say in my flesh I won't ever sin again. Yea, right! How can I, in my flesh and in my own power, do what only a born again believer can do by the power of the Holy Spirit? And only after he has been walking in the Spirit, being washed daily by the water of the Word and being renewed in the spirit of his mind.

What I'm saying is, it is impossible for anyone to change until "old things have passed away and all things become new." We didn't even know how bad we were before we received the Lord Jesus into our lives. We had no understanding of the perfect holiness of God—God dwells in the light which no sinful man can approach.

> "Who only hath immortality, dwelling in the light which no man can approach unto; whom no man hath seen, nor can see: to whom be honor and power everlasting" (1 Timothy 6:16).

What I'm saying is that repentance comes after conversion, or more specifically, starts showing itself as we grow in the Lord. Otherwise it is by our repentance that we are saved. Do you see what I mean? For example, in the prodigal son story, he was already a son. He didn't repent and then become a son.

Repentance: Seeing our own wickedness; comes after we have been with Jesus.

> "When Simon Peter saw it, he fell down at Jesus' knees, saying, Depart from me; for I am a sinful man, O Lord" (Luke 5:8).

It was only after he had been with Jesus that Peter saw his sinfulness. Biblical repentance is turning to God in faith. As we turn to God to trust Him, we take Him at His word and our faith grows. For without faith it is impossible to please God. As we are turning to God in repentance, we are also turning away from our own way and the ways of the world.

In the following Scriptures, the people believed first, then came and confessed their sins, *and then* showed their works.

> "And many that believed came, and confessed, and shewed their deeds. Many of them also which used curious arts brought their books together, and burned them before all men: and they counted the price of them, and found it fifty thousand pieces of silver" (Acts 19:18-19).

> "For they themselves showed of us what manner of entering in we had unto you, and how you turned to God from idols to serve the living and true God" (1 Thessalonians 1:9).

> "Therefore leaving the principles of the doctrine of Christ, let us go on unto perfection; not laying again the foundation of repentance from dead works, and of faith toward God" (Hebrews 6:1).

> "Wherefore my sentence is, that we trouble not them, which from among the Gentiles are turned to God" (Acts 15:19).

"Testifying both to the Jews, and also to the Greeks, repentance toward God, and faith toward our Lord Jesus Christ" (Acts 20:21).

"To open their eyes, and to turn them from darkness to light, and from the power of Satan unto God, that they may receive forgiveness of sins, and inheritance among them which are sanctified by faith that is in me" (Acts 26:18).

To repent is to turn from the power of Satan to the power of God, from darkness to light, from my way to God's way.

"But without faith it is impossible to please him: for he that cometh to God must believe that he is, and that he is a rewarder of them that diligently seek him" (Hebrews 11:6).

"But what does it say? The word is nigh thee, even in thy mouth, and in thy heart: that is, the word of faith, which we preach; that if thou shalt confess with thy mouth the Lord Jesus, and shalt believe in your heart that God hath raised him from the dead, thou shalt be saved. For with the heart man believeth unto righteousness; and with the mouth confession is made unto salvation. For the scripture says, Whoever believes on him shall not be ashamed. For there is no difference between the Jew and the Greek: for the same Lord over all is rich unto all that call upon him. For whosoever shall call upon the name of the Lord shall be saved. How then shall they call on him in whom they have not believed? and how shall they believe in him of whom they have not heard? and how shall they hear without a preacher? And how shall they preach, except they be sent? as it is written, How beautiful are the feet of them that preach the gospel of peace, and bring glad tidings of good things! But they have not all obeyed the gospel. For Isaiah said, Lord, who hath believed our report? So then faith cometh by hearing, and hearing by the word of God" (Romans 10:8-17).

"But hath in due times manifested his word through preaching, which is committed unto me according to the commandment of God our Savior" (Titus 1:3).

---

[1]W.E. Vine, *Vine's Expository Dictionary of Old & New Testament Words* (Nashville, TN: Thomas Nelson, 2003).

9

CLEAR, SIMPLE PRESENTATION

In Cork City, Ireland, as I was looking for "lost sheep," I came upon four teenage boys who, after I shared the gospel, joyfully received the Lord. I encouraged them to share their experience with their friends, exhorting them with John 8:31-32, "Jesus said, If you continue in my word, then you shall be my disciples indeed; you shall know the truth, and the truth shall make you free." One of them asked, "How long will you be here?" I said, "A couple of hours." He said, "Good."

A half-hour later they came back with twenty-five other friends, all boys except for two young teenage girls. When I started to share the gospel with them, four of the boys said that one of the two girls was a sinner. I said we all have sinned and come short of the glory of God. But the girl was so embarrassed she walked away. I continued sharing the Word of God and all of them received the Lord. They left and soon brought back ten more friends, all teenage girls. As I started to present the gospel to them, a boy began screaming behind me and I could not get him to be quiet. The girls said to shout as loudly as I could so they could hear the gospel, and I did. All the girls received the Lord.

Then from around the corner, the young girl who had left embarrassed returned and said to me, "Mister, if I prayed to receive the Lord in my mind, but I was serious, did Jesus come in my heart also…and forgive me for all my sins?" She was standing down the street and she heard everything because I had to yell over the boy that was screaming. Praise the Lord! God had a way for this little girl to hear the good news, believe the gospel, and say the sinner's prayer.

In presenting the gospel, we need to remember that it must be simple enough for even a child to understand. Jesus said in Mark 10:14-15, "Allow the little children to come to Me, and do not forbid them; for of such is the kingdom of God. Truly, truly, I say to you, whosoever shall not receive the kingdom of God as a little child, he shall not enter into it." Also remember that this is a spiritual event. We are not trying to convince their intellect; we are speaking past their intellect to their spirit. We want to plant the Word of God in their heart, sowing to their spirit so that the Holy Spirit can do the job of convicting them of their sin.

"And when He (the Holy Spirit) is come, He will reprove the world of sin, and of righteousness, and of judgment" (John 16:8).

SHEPHERD'S VOICE

These are the five Scriptures I mentioned in Chapter Four. I just quote them straight from the Word of God and they work!

1. Jesus answered and said unto him, "Truly, truly, I say unto you, Except a man be born again, he cannot see the kingdom of God" (John 3:3).

2. Jesus said unto him, "I am the way, the truth, and the life: no man can come to the Father, but by Me" (John 14:6).

3. "But as many as received Him, to them He gave power to become the sons of God, even to them that believe on His name" (John 1:12).

4. "For the wages of sin is death; but the gift of God is eternal life through Jesus Christ our Lord" (Romans 6:23).

5. Jesus said to those Jews who believed on Him, "If you continue in My word, then you shall be My disciples indeed; you will know the truth, and the truth shall make you free" (John 8:31-32).

SIMPLE INVITATION

After I share the first four Scriptures with them, I ask them to pray with me to receive Jesus Christ into their life as their Lord and Savior for the forgiveness of all their sins. Then I share the fifth verse to exhort them to get in the Word.

How do you know if they are serious? You don't know and it is not your job to know. It's God's business. "But I don't want false conversions," you say. God help them if it was you who converted them. I believe it is the Holy Spirit that is doing the work in their heart.

> "That if you will confess with your mouth the Lord Jesus, and will believe in your heart that God hath raised Him from the dead, you shalt be saved" (Romans 10:9).

> "But Jesus called them unto him, and said, Allow the little children to come unto me, and forbid them not: for of such is the kingdom of God. Truly I say unto you, Whosoever shall not receive the kingdom of God as a little child shall in no wise enter therein" (Luke 18:16-17).

They must believe by faith, faith as a little child. Faith comes by hearing and hearing by the Word of God. Do not try to convince their intellect. It is not intellectual; it is spiritual.

> "It is the spirit that makes alive; the flesh profits nothing: the words that I speak unto you, they are spirit, and they are life" (John 6:63).

"And it came to pass, as he sowed, some fell by the way side, and the birds of the air came and devoured it up. And some fell on stony ground, where it had not much earth; and immediately it sprang up, because it had no depth of earth: But when the sun was up, it was scorched; and because it had no root, it withered away. And some fell among thorns, and the thorns grew up, and choked it, and it yielded no fruit. And other fell on good ground, and did yield fruit that sprang up and increased; and brought forth, some thirty, and some sixty, and some an hundredfold. And he said unto them, He that hath ears to hear, let him hear" (Mark 4:4-9).

In a farming society they would understand this parable. From a city background we would think 25% is attributed for each type of soil, meaning most (75%) is worthless! To those people that Jesus was talking to, they would understand that just a small amount would land on the wayside, a small amount would fall on the stony ground, and a certain amount would fall among weeds. That leaves the majority falling on the possibly good soil. Jesus said the harvest is truly ripe, but the laborers are few! Pray to the Lord of the harvest to send forth more laborers.

We are to preach the gospel using the Word of God, whether we are planting, watering or reaping. But God's Word never tells us to try to determine what type of soil they are because their soil condition can change. We are not soil checkers, but sowers and fishermen. We cast out the seed—the Word of God—we water the seed, but God gives the increase.

If someone says they believe in Jesus, that they have asked Him into their heart and they are letting God be the Lord of their life, don't doubt it. We should always rejoice with the angels of God over one sinner that comes to repentance. Our job in the body of Christ is to pray and intercede for the new believers to be filled daily with the Holy Spirit, for God to speak to them through His Word. Don't grill them on what they believe. Don't try to make sure they have all the doctrines down. Just encourage them to read God's Word daily, to have fellowship with Him, and to do what He tells them to do in His Word—to let Jesus be the Lord of their life.

> "Then said he unto his disciples, The harvest truly is plenteous, but the laborers are few; pray ye therefore the Lord of the harvest, that he will send forth laborers into his harvest" (Matthew 9:37-38).

1 0

ADVICE TO GIVE TO NEW BELIEVERS

"Jesus said to those Jews which believed on Him, if you continue in my Word, then you shall be my disciples indeed; you will know the truth, and the truth shall make you free" (John 8:31-32).

This is a very important Scripture to share with a new believer. Speak it to them and the Holy Spirit will use it to remind them to continue in the Lord. Remember that God's Word does not return void.

"For my thoughts are not your thoughts, neither are your ways my ways, saith the LORD. For as the heavens are higher than the earth, so are my ways higher than your ways, and my thoughts than your thoughts. For as the rain cometh down, and the snow from heaven, and returneth not thither, but watereth the earth, and maketh it bring forth and bud, that it may give seed to the sower, and bread to the eater: So shall my word be that goeth forth out of my mouth: it shall not return unto me void, but it shall accomplish that which I please, and it shall prosper in the thing whereto I sent it" (Isaiah 55:8-11).

To encourage new believers in their walk with the Lord, I tell them:

• Read the Bible every day.

• Make sure to pray and ask God to speak to you through His Word.

• Be sure it is quiet when you read the Word of God, so when He talks to you, you can hear Him.

• Have a notebook to journal what God shows you. Pray for God to help you do what He says.

• When you pray, talk to God right from your heart and give God time to talk to you.

Sometimes a new believer will ask which church to go to. I tell them the name of the church isn't important; the important thing is, do they believe the Bible is the inspired Word of God? And do they teach it as such? Does the church body live by the Word of God personally?

And now, the most important thing—you have friends, right? Some of your friends have Jesus in their hearts already, and others don't. You can't tell just by looking at them, so you have to ask them. And if they don't have Jesus in their hearts, pray with them. Now don't force them, but try to bring as many people to heaven with you as you can. It's the only thing that will make any difference when we get to heaven. And in your friend's life, it will make an eternity of difference.

Now some of your friends will laugh at you. Expect it. But some of your friends will say they have wanted to know God personally all their life and they will thank you for sharing with them. You know, some of those who laughed at you at first will come to you later to pray to receive the Lord.

After I have shared the Word of God with people, I ask them if they want to go to heaven when they die. If they say yes, I tell them that first they must believe that Jesus Christ died on the cross for all of their sins, and after three days God raised Him from the dead. I ask, "Do you believe that?" If they say yes, then I say, "I'll pray with you now to receive Jesus Christ into your life to be your Lord and Savior for the forgiveness of all your sins and to guide your life." Then I lead them in prayer. Share in a way that your friends will not feel offended by the way you present the gospel to them, but are actually happy about how you shared without putting pressure on them to believe. My hope is that this little book will help you, whether you have been evangelizing for years or have been so timid you are still waiting to tell your first person.

MY PRAYER

Father, I pray for all believers. I pray that Your Holy Spirit would fall afresh on us. Speak to us through Your Word, guide us in prayer and fellowship, lead us to church, search us and know our hearts, try us and know our ways, and see if there be any wicked way in us and lead us in the way everlasting. And Lord, help us to share Your gospel with others today. In Jesus' name, amen.

For more information on Shepherd's Voice, future publications, and to see demonstrations of evangelism, go to www.shepherdsvoice.com and click on the videos provided for training.

Steve has taken over 150 missions trips worldwide and is available to conduct missions and evangelism training entitled, "Evangelism for Dummies."

He may be contacted at steve@shepherdsvoice.com

TAKE IT WITH ME SCRIPTURE VERSES

Jesus answered and said unto him, Verily, verily, I say unto thee, Except a man be born again, he cannot see the kingdom of God. (John 3:3)

Jesus saith unto him, I am the way, the truth, and the life: no man cometh unto the Father, but by me. (John 14:6)

But as many as received him, to them gave he power to become the sons of God, even to them that believe on his name. (John 1:12)

For the wages of sin is death; but the gift of God is eternal life through Jesus Christ our Lord. (Romans 6:23)

If they say yes, pray with them and then read the following verse:

Then said Jesus to those Jews which believed on him, If ye continue in my word, then are ye my disciples indeed; and ye shall know the truth, and the truth shall make you free. (John 8:31-32)